Thanks to park ranger Werner Van Hove.

Copyright © 2021 Clavis Publishing Inc., New York

Originally published as *De boswachter* in Belgium and the Netherlands by Clavis Uitgeverij, 2020
English translation from the Dutch by Clavis Publishing Inc., New York

Visit us on the Web at www.clavis-publishing.com.

Park Rangers and What They Do written and illustrated by Liesbet Slegers

ISBN 978-1-60537-714-8

This book was printed in April 2021 at Nikara, M. R. Štefánika 858/25, 963 01 Krupina, Slovakia.

First Edition
10 9 8 7 6 5 4 3 2 1

Clavis Publishing supports the First Amendment and celebrates the right to read.

Park Rangers
and What They Do

Liesbet Slegers

Clavis

NEW YORK

The management plan shows what the forest should look like now and later.

It's nice to take a walk in the forest and discover beautiful places.
There's a lot to see and hear! Are there any trees with dead branches
that can fall onto the trail? Did any rare animals pass by?
The park ranger keeps an eye on it all. She also carries out
the management plan. Is it necessary to plant extra tree species?
Or are there trees that have to go? The park ranger has her own tools.
But she also cooperates with forestry workers, who have big machines.
Do you want to come along through the forest, together with the park ranger?

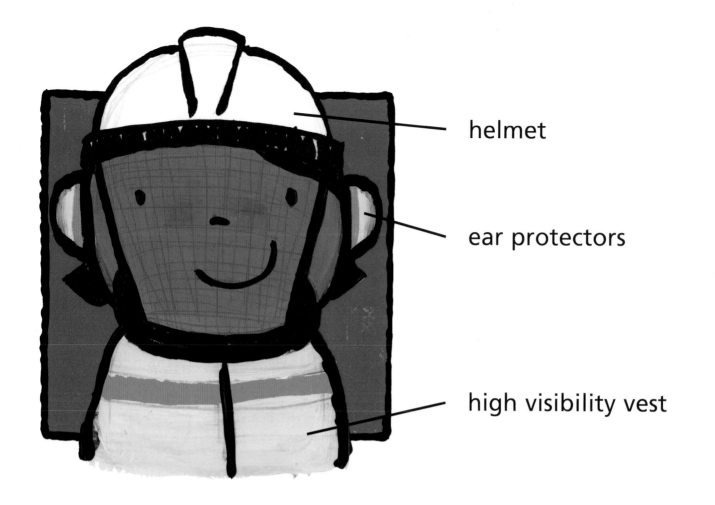

helmet

ear protectors

high visibility vest

The park ranger wears **clothes** in the **colors of the forest**: shades of brown and green. Smart! That way, she doesn't stand out between the trees and she doesn't disturb the animals. The park ranger always wears **long pants with pockets** and **sturdy hiking boots**, even in summer. That way, her legs and feet are protected from mosquitoes, ticks, or other animals that sting. Attached to a **special belt**, the park ranger carries her tools. In case of dangerous work, the park ranger wears a **helmet** and **ear protection**. The **safety vest**, which does stand out, is used by the park ranger when she works at the edge of the forest, next to a busy highway, for instance. On wet, swampy ground, the park ranger wears **rain boots**.

park ranger's hat

park ranger's clothes

belt with tools

rain boots

warm winter coat

sturdy hiking boots

The night camera can make a video in the dark when an animal passes by!

Various tools are attached to the belt: a **small** and a **big flashlight**, and a handy **pocketknife**. With **binoculars**, not only can the park ranger see animals better, but also danger. In **animal and plant guidebooks**, she can look up rare species. With her **smartphone**, the park ranger photographs animal tracks: maybe a wolf or a beaver passed by? The **GPS** helps her find her way, and of course, the park ranger also has to be able to make a call. The **night camera** shoots footage of animals that pass by at night. In the **management plan**, the park ranger reads what the forest should look like now and in the future. With the **caliper**, she measures the thickness of a tree trunk, with the **altimeter**, she measures the height of a tree. And with the **marking axe**, she puts a stamp on the trees that have to be cut down.

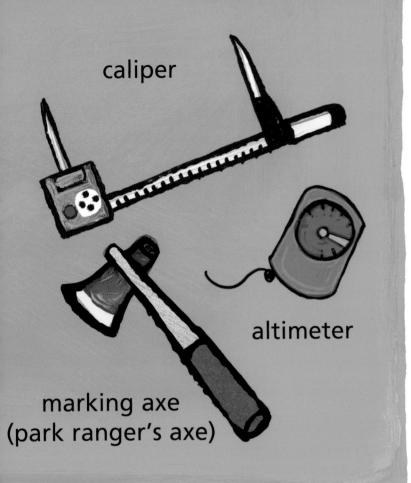

caliper

altimeter

marking axe
(park ranger's axe)

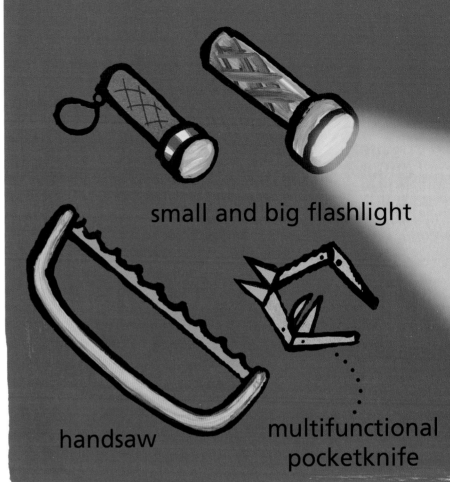

small and big flashlight

handsaw

multifunctional
pocketknife

laptop

smartphone
with GPS

management plan

binoculars

animal and plant guidebooks

Last night, the park ranger was sleeping peacefully.
Suddenly, the wind started to blow, and it started to rain heavily.
A violent storm broke out with thunder and lightning!
The next morning, the park ranger wakes up early, and thinks
of her forest. Hopefully, not many trees were blown over last night . . .
She quickly answers a few questions on her laptop and calls the workers
that are coming to the forest today. Then she puts on her park ranger's
clothes, grabs her material, and heads out. After that storm,
it's going to be a busy day in the forest today!

The park ranger walks her route through the forest.
One big tree fell over. It's lying on the trail now.
A bit further on, she also sees a thick branch torn off.
The park ranger calls the forestry workers, who are also
already at work in the forest, "Can you saw the tree into pieces
and remove it?" The park ranger passes on the location of the fallen tree.
With her little handsaw, she clears up the torn off branch herself.

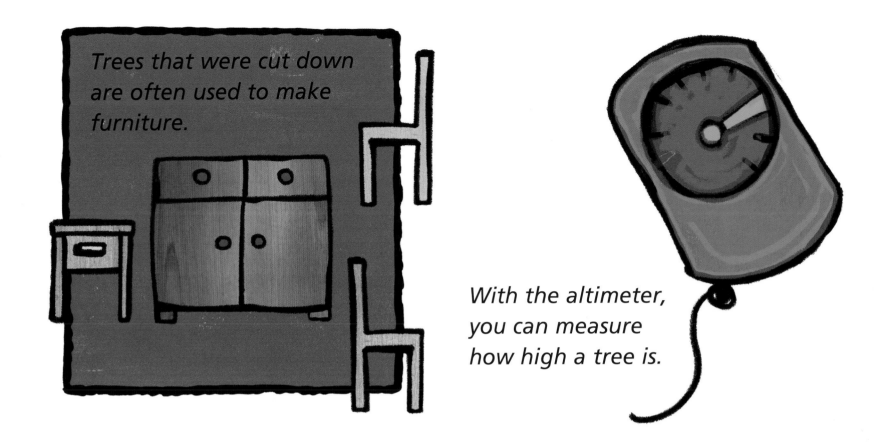

Trees that were cut down are often used to make furniture.

With the altimeter, you can measure how high a tree is.

A bit further on in the forest, the park ranger has another job to do. She's taken a good look at her forest management plan. In this place, beautiful oaks have been growing for hundreds of years. This has to stay that way. So, the other tree species growing can't stay here. After they're cut down, new, young oaks are planted here.

First, the park ranger measures the trees that have to go. With the caliper, she finds out exactly how thick a tree is. When she measures the height with the altimeter, she knows how much money can be earned by selling the wood of this tree. Later, wooden furniture is made out of the tree.

This is a future tree. That's a tree that has to stay forever. With a special spray can, the park ranger puts blue dots on the tree trunk. Everyone who works in the forest knows what those dots mean. Smart!

There, the measuring is done. Now the park ranger has to mark the tree. That way, the workers can see which trees can be cut down and which can't. She has a special axe for that: the marking axe. With the axe side, she chips away some bark. After that, she slams a stamp into the bare, soft wood with the stamp side. That way, the park ranger makes sure that the forestry workers know which trees have to go: all trees with this stamp will be cut down soon.

Sometimes, the park ranger sees rare birds through her binoculars. In her bird guidebook, she can look up which species is singing so beautifully!

There, that job is done. Suddenly, she hears a birdsong that she doesn't recognize. Quickly, she grabs her binoculars. Wow, she hasn't seen that bird species around here very often yet. Maybe new beetles that this bird likes to eat are living in the forest. She'll investigate that later. But first, she walks over to the night camera. It's hanging in this place because deer often cross the trail here. Did the camera shoot some footage of deer last night? Or maybe a wolf, a fox, or a beaver was seen? Or maybe nothing at all . . .

Do you help to take care of a forest by not leaving trash? Don't throw away your trash in nature, but in a trash can!

The park ranger walks further over the trail. Oh no, what happened here? A big pile of trash was dumped. How awful! Who would have done this? The park ranger notes down what happened: she makes a report, just like the police do, and takes pictures. Maybe someone has seen something? She'll certainly sort it out. But now, she has to meet the forestry workers first. Later, when she comes back, she'll send someone to pick up the trash.

The grass, which is far too long, is mowed first.

The park ranger arrives at an open area without trees, where forestry workers are already busy. Here, only grass grows, which was way too long. The grass has been mowed already, but it needs to be even shorter. That's why a farmer from the neighborhood will bring his flock of sheep to graze. But first, the forestry workers install an enclosure, so the sheep won't get lost in the forest later on.

Here comes the farmer with his sheep. How funny, sheep in the forest!
Hey, there's a donkey too. Of course, he also likes grass. The park ranger
checks everything thoroughly. Is the enclosure okay? Do the animals feel
good here? She thanks the forestry workers for the enclosure.
Now the sheep and the donkey can graze calmly. Delicious for them
and good for the forest! Soon, the grass will be very short and then
the animals can go back to the farm.

A nature walk in the forest has been planned for that night.
Grown-ups and children walk through the forest in the dark together
with the park ranger. Exciting! If they're very quiet and don't disrupt
the animals, they might see a snout of a porcupine or hear the beautiful
tawny owl call: hoot! – hoot!

Thank you, park ranger, for taking care of the forest and protecting
nature. That way, the forest is and remains a nice place for the trees
and animals that live there. And of course, also for the people who
come to visit!

Take a guess, does the park ranger do these activities in spring, summer, autumn or winter?

The park ranger runs into a hiker. This man has picked many mushrooms. He wants to sell them. The park ranger says he isn't allowed to do that. The mushrooms have to stay where they are. They're necessary in the forest because they clear up the fallen leaves.

In autumn

It's hot. The park ranger looks at the butterflies flying over the field. Are there many of one specific species? And of which species are there none? By watching the butterflies and by counting them, the park ranger finds out a lot about the flowers and the plants here. And also whether the field may be getting too dry.

In summer